Disclaimer

This book is designed solely for educational purposes. The tricks and mnemonic techniques provided are intended to assist learners in memorizing articles of the Indian Constitution more effectively.

While we may reference certain brand names as part of these techniques, such references are used purely as educational tools and are not intended to imply endorsement, affiliation, or any commercial relationship with the respective brands. All brand names and trademarks remain the property of their respective owners.

This book and its contents are not intended for legal use, and they cannot be presented or relied upon in any court of law against the authors or publishers.

We have made every effort to ensure the accuracy and appropriateness of the content. However, the authors and publishers disclaim any liability for any misunderstandings, misinterpretations, or misuse of the content provided in this book.

Tricks to Remember Articles of the Indian Constitution

Table of Contents

Acknowledgement

I extend my heartfelt gratitude to all those who have contributed to the making of this book. Firstly, I would like to express my deepest appreciation to my mentors and teachers whose guidance and support have been invaluable throughout my journey of preparing for the UPSC and state PCS examinations. Their wisdom and encouragement have been instrumental in shaping my understanding of the Indian Constitution.

I am also indebted to my family and friends for their unwavering support and encouragement during the ups and downs of my preparation. Their belief in me has been a constant source of motivation.

Additionally, I would like to thank the authors and scholars whose works I have consulted and drawn inspiration from in the process of creating this book. Their insights have enriched my understanding of the subject matter.

Lastly, I am grateful to the aspirants and students who have provided feedback and suggestions, helping me refine and improve the content of this book.

This book is a culmination of collective efforts, and I am sincerely thankful to everyone who has played a part, directly or indirectly, in its creation.

Introduction

Welcome to "Tricks to Remember Articles of the Indian Constitution," a comprehensive guide crafted to ease the daunting task of memorizing the intricate details of one of the world's lengthiest and most complex constitutional documents. Authored with the aim of aiding aspirants preparing for competitive examinations such as the UPSC and state PCS, this book offers innovative mnemonic devices, practical memory aids, and insightful explanations to facilitate your journey toward mastery of the Indian Constitution.

Understanding the Indian Constitution is not just a requirement for examinations; it is essential for anyone seeking to comprehend the foundations of India's democracy and governance. However, the sheer volume of articles and provisions can often overwhelm aspirants, leading to frustration and disarray. This book aims to alleviate those challenges by providing effective techniques and strategies to make the learning process both efficient and enjoyable.

In this introduction, we will explore the importance of memorizing the articles of the Indian Constitution and provide an overview of the approach taken in this book. By the end of this introduction, you will have a clear understanding of how this book can support your journey toward success in competitive examinations and beyond.

Let's embark on this enlightening journey together, as we unravel the complexities of the Indian Constitution and equip ourselves with the knowledge and skills needed to excel in our endeavors.

Shall we begin?

How to use this book

1.Learn the Code: Familiarize yourself with the numerical associations for consonants. For instance, '0' corresponds to 'Z' and 'S', '1' to 'T' and 'D', and so on. These associations will form the foundation of your mnemonic toolkit.

2.Encode the Articles: As you study the articles of the Indian Constitution, encode them using the provided numerical associations. For example, if Article 15 pertains to prohibition of discrimination on grounds of religion, race, caste, sex, or place of birth, you might encode it as "1RL".

3.Connect with Vowels: To form complete words, incorporate vowels that match the consonants in your code. For instance, "1RL" could translate to "Trail" or "Drill". This step adds a layer of vividness to your memory associations.

4.Practice and Reinforce: Regularly review and practice recalling the encoded articles using the code and associated words. Over time, these mnemonic devices will become second nature, enabling you to effortlessly recall and understand the provisions of the Indian Constitution.

With "The Constitution Codebook," navigating the complexities of India's governance framework becomes a fascinating journey of discovery and memorization. Unlock the secrets of the Constitution and empower yourself with a deeper understanding of India's legal landscape.

Left Blank

Number table

Numbers	Alphabets
0	Z , S
1	T, D
2	N
3	M
4	R
5	L
6	G, J, Ch, Sh
7	K,C
8	F, V
9	P, B

Note :-

Below are the vowels that should not be considered if used in the words attached to the above alphabets.

"a, e, i , o, u"

<u>**Important note:**</u> Omitted articles note has not been create if you wish you can apply the method given in this book and make tricks for the omitted ones.

Some articles have numbers and Alphabets, for such articles we will use US navy phonetics. Which given below:

- **A**: Alpha
- **B**: Bravo
- **C**: Charlie
- **D**: Delta
- **E**: Echo
- **F**: Foxtrot
- **G**: Golf
- **H**: Hotel
- **I**: India
- **J**: Juliet
- **K**: Kilo
- **L**: Lima
- **M**: Mike
- **N**: November
- **O**: Oscar
- **P**: Papa

- **Q**: Quebec
- **R**: Romeo
- **S**: Sierra
- **T**: Tango
- **U**: Uniform
- **V**: Victor
- **W**: Whiskey
- **X**: X-ray
- **Y**: Yankee
- **Z**: Zulu

Article No.	Article Information	Trick to Remember
PART I **THE UNION AND ITS TERRITORY**		
1	Name and territory of the Union.	Tau ne India ka naam aur territory di hai union ke liye.
2	Admission or establishment of new States.	Nao se hum naye state jate hai
3	Formation of new States and alteration of areas, boundaries or names of existing States.	*Maa states ke boundaries aur areas mein badlaav laa sakti hai.*
4	Laws made under articles 2 and 3 to provide for the amendment of the First and the Fourth Schedules and supplemental, incidental and consequential matters	URI attack has made law under article 2 & 3 for amending 1st and 4th Schedules.
PART II **CITIZENSHIP**		
5	Citizenship at the commencement of the Constitution.	Lao constituton bano Citizen.
6	Rights of citizenship of certain persons who have migrated to India from Pakistan.	Sai ne Pakistan se India aaye logo ko

		citizenship ka rights diya
7	Rights of citizenship of certain migrants to Pakistan.	Kia ne kuch Pakistan hue migrants ko citizenship ka rights diya.
8	Rights of citizenship of certain persons of Indian origin residing outside India.	Rights of citizenship Via Indian origin residing outside india.
9	Persons voluntarily acquiring citizenship of a foreign State not to be citizen.	OoP! You have voluntarily acquired foreign state now you are not a Indian citizen.
10	Continuance of the rights of citizenship.	DaSi will continue the rights of citizenship.
11	Parliament to regulate the right of citizenship by law.	TeD in paliament will regulate right of citizenship by law

PART III
FUNDAMENTAL RIGHTS

12	Definition.	TooN Defines fundamental rights
13	Laws inconsistent with or in derogation of the fundamental rights.	TeaM made law in derogation of fundamental rights

Right to Equality

14	Equality before law.	DooR should be equal before law

Article	Provision	Memory Trick
15	Prohibition of discrimination on grounds of religion, race, caste, sex or place of birth.	Caste, Gender etc are TooL for discrimination.
16	Equality of opportunity in matters of public employment.	DoG has equal opportunity in public employment.
17	Abolition of Untouchability.	Take untouchability
18	Abolition of titles.	Title on TV
	Right to Freedom	
19	Protection of certain rights regarding freedom of speech, etc.	**6 freedom trick:** If you speak with expression and Assemble peacefully without arms in front of association or union, then you are free to move and settle and practice any profession. **Article trick** TaP to freedom
20	Protection in respect of conviction for offences.	NoSe can convict you for offences
21	Protection of life and personal liberty.	NoDi has protection of life and personal liberty.
21A	Right to education.	NeT Aplha has educational right.

22	Protection against arrest and detention in certain cases.	NoNe can protect you against arrest and detain in certain cases.
	Right against Exploitation	
23	Prohibition of traffic in human beings and forced labour.	NaaM ke majdoor traffic par kam kar rahe hai.
24	Prohibition of employment of children in factories, etc.	NRi kids will not work in factory.
25	Freedom of conscience and free profession, practice and propagation of religion.	NaiL & coin are for religious practice.
26	Freedom to manage religious affairs.	NaaG manage religious affairs
27	Freedom as to payment of taxes for promotion of any particular religion.	NaaK me dum kar diya hai religous tax promote karte karte.
28	Freedom as to attendance at religious instruction or religious worship in certain educational institutions.	NiFe always follow relgious instruction.
	Cultural and Educational Rights	
29	Protection of interests of minorities.	NooB protect interests of minorities.

30	Right of minorities to establish and administer educational institutions.	MouSe establish and administer educational institutions.
	Saving of Certain Laws	
31A	Saving of Laws providing for acquisition of estates, etc.	MooD Apha decides to save laws providing for acquisition of estates.
31B	Validation of certain Acts and Regulations.	MooD ka Beta validates certain acts and regulations.
31C	Saving of laws giving effect to certain directive principles.	MooD Ka Charlie saves laws giving effect to certain directive principles.
	Right to Constitutional Remedies	
32	Remedies for enforcement of fundamental rights	MooN has remedy to enforce fundamental rights
33	Power of Parliament to modify the fundamental rights in their application to Forces, etc.	MaaM has power to modify fundamental rights.
34	Restriction on fundamental rights while martial law is in force in any area.	MR. Your fundamental rights are restricted in martial law.
35	Legislation to give effect to the provisions of Fundamental rights.	MooLi of Legislation give effect to provisoins of FR.
	PART IV DIRECTIVE PRINCIPLES OF STATE POLICY	

36	Definition Of State	MauG is the definition of state
37	Application of the directive principles .	MiKe gave application to DPSP
38	State to secure a social order for the promotion of welfare of the people.	MooVe social order to promote welfare of the people in state.
39	Certain principles of policy to be followed by the State.	MoB has certain principles of policy to be followed by states.
39A	Equal justice and free legal aid.	MaP Alpha to get equal justice & free legal Aid.
40	Organisation of village panchayats.	RoSe used to organize village panchayats.
41	Right to work, to education and to public assistance in certain cases.	RaT can work & get education and give public assistance.
42	Provision for just and humane conditions of work and maternity relief.	RuN for just work conditions and maternity relief.
43	Living wage, etc., for workers.	RooM for living on wage for Worker
43A	Participation of workers in management of industries.	RoMa and Alpha can allow workers participation in management of industries.
43B	Promotion of co-operative societies.	RoMa Beta Got promotion in co-operative societies.

44	Uniform civil code for the citizens.	RaR files have Uniform Civil Code.
45	Provision for early childhood care and education to children below the age of six years.	RaiL has provision for early childhood care and education for children below 6.
46	Promotion of educational and economic interests of Scheduled Castes, Scheduled Tribes and other weaker sections.	RJ is promoting educational & economical interest of SC, ST and other weaker sections.
47	Duty of the State to raise the level of nutrition and the standard of living and to improve public health.	RooK in state raise the leve of nutrition and std. of living to improve health.
48	Organisation of agriculture and animal husbandry.	Ravi has Organisation of agriculture and animal husbandry.
48A	Protection and improvement of environment and safeguarding of forests and wild life.	Ravi and Alpha Protect environment, forest and wildlife.
49	Protection of monuments and places and objects of national importance.	RiP Monuments, places & object of International Importance.
50	Separation of judiciary from executive.	LooSe Connection seperates Judiciary from Executive.
51	Promotion of international peace and security.	Play LuDo to promote international peace and Security.

PART IVA

FUNDAMENTAL DUTIES

51A	Fundamental duties.	LoaD Alpha with fundamental duties.

PART V
THE UNION
CHAPTER 1 - THE EXECUTIVE
The President and Vice-President

Article	Description	Mnemonic
52	The President of India.	Indian President is LioN.
53	Executive power of the Union.	Drink LiMe Juice to get Executive power of Union.
54	Election of President.	LiaR declares election of President.
55	Manner of election of President.	LuLu shows no manners in election of President.
56	Term of office of President.	LOG terminal of President office. Note: Terminal denote – Term.
57	Eligibility for re-election.	Look eligibility for re-election
58	Qualifications for election as President.	LoVe my qualification for election as president.
59	Conditions of President's office.	LooP conditions of president's office
60	Oath or affirmation by the President.	GoD supervise Oath or affirmation by president.
61	Procedure for impeachment of the President.	GoT the procedure to remove president.

62	Time of holding election to fill vacancy in the office of President and the term of office of person elected to fill casual vacancy.	GuN borrow time of holding election to fill vacancy in president office.
63	The Vice-President of India.	Indian Vice President eats only JaM
64	The Vice-President to be ex officio Chairman of the Council of States.	Vice-President kept JaR inside council of state for ex-officio chairman.
65	The Vice-President to act as President or to discharge his functions during casual vacancies in the office, or during the absence, of President.	Put vice-President in JaiL to act as president.
66	Election of Vice-President.	My JiJa stood in the election of Vice-President.
67	Term of office of Vice-President.	GeeK knows Term of office of Vice-President.
68	Time of holding election to fill vacancy in the office of Vice-President and the term of office of person elected to fill casual vacancy.	GiF takes time for holding election to fill vacancy in the office of vice-president.
69	Oath or affirmation by the Vice-President.	JoB witness Oath or affirmation by the vice-president.
70	Discharge of President's functions in other contingencies.	CaSe discharge president's function in other contigencies.

71	Matters relating to, or connected with, the election of a President or Vice-President.	CaT has matter related to election of a president or vice-president.
72	Power of President to grant pardons, etc., and to suspend, remit or commute sentences in certain cases.	KauN Pardon karega Mr. President?
73	Extent of executive power of the Union.	CoMe and extend the executive power of the Union.
	Council of Ministers	
74	Council of Ministers to aid and advise President.	Council of ministers advice KaRo president ko.
75	Other provisions as to Ministers.	CooL to have other provision as to ministers.
	The Attorney-General for India	
76	Attorney-General for India.	1.Aapne India ke Attorney-General ko KG ki knowledge honi chahiye. 2. AGI ko KG me bhejo). Note: you can use any one of the above tricks to memorize it.
	Conduct of Government Business	

77	Conduct of business of the Government of India.	Cook to conduct the business of the GOI.
78	Duties of Prime Minister as respects the furnishing of information to the President, etc.	CaVe noted the duties of Prime Minister as respects the furnishing of information to the President, etc.

CHAPTER 2 - PARLIAMENT

79	Constitution of Parliament.	Always KeeP constitution of Parliament.
80	Composition of the Council of States(Rajya Sabha).	FaiZu compose song on Rajya Sabha.
81	Composition of the House of the People(Lok Sabha).	FaT people compose Lok Sabha.
82	Readjustment after each census.	FaN do readjustment after each census.
83	Duration of Houses of Parliament.	Need FaMe to decide Duration of house of Parliament.
84	Qualification for membership of Parliament.	FaiR qualification required for membership of parliament.
85	Sessions of Parliament, prorogation and dissolution.	FooL the sessions of parliament prorogation and dissolution.
86	Right of President to address and send messages to Houses.	VaGue right of president to address and send messages to houses.

87	Special address by the President.	FaKe special address by the president.
88	Rights of Ministers and Attorney-General as respects Houses.	FuFa has rights of ministers and Attorney-General as respects Houses.

Officers of Parliament

89	The Chairman and Deputy Chairman of the Council of States.	ViPe the chairman and Deputy chairman of the council of States.
90	Vacation and resignation of, and removal from, the office of Deputy Chairman.	BooSe during vacation or resignation of the office of deputy chairman.
91	Power of the Deputy Chairman or other person to perform the duties of the office of, or to act as, Chairman.	BooT has power of the deputy chairman to act as chairman.
92	The Chairman or the Deputy Chairman not to preside while a resolution for his removal from office is under consideration.	BaN the chairman or deputy chairman to preside while his removal from office is under consideration.
93	The Speaker and Deputy Speaker of the House of the People.	PuMa company has Speaker and Deputy speaker in his house of people.
94	Vacation and resignation of, and removal from, the offices of Speaker and Deputy Speaker.	PooR vacate and remove office of speaker and deputy speaker.

95	Power of the Deputy Speaker or other person to perform the duties of the office of, or to act as, Speaker.	BaiL gives power to deputy speaker to act as speaker.
96	The Speaker or the Deputy Speaker not to preside while a resolution for his removal from office is under consideration.	PiG said speaker and deputy speaker cannot preside when removal from office is under consideration.
97	Salaries and allowances of the Chairman and Deputy Chairman and the Speaker and Deputy Speaker.	BooK salaries and allowances of chairman, deputy charman, speaker and Deputy speaker.
98	Secretariat of Parliament.	BF is the secretariat of Parliament.

Conduct of Business

99	Oath or affirmation by members.	PaaPi needsOath and Affirmation by members to conduct business.
100	Voting in Houses, power of Houses to act notwithstanding vacancies and quorum.	ToSS for voting in house and for power to act notwithstanding vacancies and quorum.

Disqualifications of Members

101	Vacation of seats.	DuST on Vacant of seats due to disqualification.

102	Disqualifications for membership.	DoZeN listed under Disqualifications for membership.
103	Decision on questions as to disqualifications of members.	DoSuM to make decision on disqualifications of members.
104	Penalty for sitting and voting before making oath or affirmation under article 99 or when not qualified or when disqualified.	TeaSeR me penalty bhi hai agar bina oath liye vote kiya to ya disqualify hai to.

Powers, Privileges and Immunities of Parliament and its Members

105	Powers, privileges, etc., of the Houses of Parliament and of the members and committees thereof.	TaSLa gives power & privilege to the members and committees of Parliament.
106	Salaries and allowances of members.	DoSaGe of salaries and allowances are required for parliament members.

Legislative Procedure

107	Provisions as to introduction and passing of Bills.	DoZaK has provision to introduce and passing of bills
108	Joint sitting of both Houses in certain cases.	TaSVo park has joint sitting of both houses in certain cases.
109	Special procedure in respect of Money Bills.	DSP knows special procedure in respect of Money bill.

| 110 | Definition of "Money Bills". | TaTooS Defines Money bill |
| 111 | Assent to Bills. | D-To-D sends Assent to bills. |

Procedure in Financial Matters

112	Annual financial statement.	TuTioN me we always read Anual financial statement.
113	Procedure in Parliament with respect to estimates.	DaDiMa knows the procedure w.r.t financial estimates in parliament.
114	Appropriation Bills.	DaDaR station ko aapropriate bill se banaya hai.
115	Supplementary, additional or excess grants.	TiTLi needs supplementary excess grants.
116	Votes on account, votes of credit and exceptional grants.	DaDaJi can vote on account, credit and exceptional grants.
117	Special provisions as to financial Bills.	TuTaK provides special provisions to financial bills.

Procedure Generally

| 118 | Rules of procedure. | TaTVa gyan se rule of prcedure paida hota hai. |
| 119 | Regulation by law of procedure in Parliament in relation to financial business. | TaDaP because of regulation by law has procedure in parliament related to financial business. |

120	Language to be used in Parliament.	TaNSe language to be used in parliament.
121	Restriction on discussion in Parliament.	DeNT restrict on discussion in parliament.
122	Courts not to inquire into proceedings of Parliament.	DiNaN ke hit ke liye court parliament ke proceeding me inquire nahi kar sakta.

CHAPTER 3 - LEGISLATIVE POWERS OF THE PRESIDENT

123	Power of President to promulgate Ordinances during recess of Parliament.	DeNiM powers the president to promulgate Ordinances during recess of Parliament.

CHAPTER 4 - THE UNION JUDICIARY

124	Establishment and constitution of Supreme Court.	DoNaR Established supreme court constitution.
124A	National Judicial Appointments Commission.	DoNaR(or DiNaR) Alpha ko National judicial Appointmemts commission mila hai.
124B	Functions of Commission.	DoNaR(or DiNaR) Beta ko commission ke functions mile hai.
124C	Power of Parliament to make law.	DoNaR(or DiNaR) Charlie ne parliament ko power diya hai law banane ke liye.
125	Salaries, etc., of Judges.	DoNaL pays salaries of Judges.

126	Appointment of acting Chief Justice.	DoNaLi leke acting chief justice appoint karte hai.
127	Appointment of ad hoc judges.	TaNK Appoints ad hoc judges.
128	Attendance of retired Judges at sittings of the Supreme Court.	DaNaV took attendance of retired Judgest at sittings of the supreme court.
129	Supreme Court to be a court of record.	TaNPe likh liya ki supreme court is a court of record.
130	Seat of Supreme Court.	DiMS seats of supreme court.
131	Original jurisdiction of the Supreme Court.	ToMaTo has original jurisdiction of the Supreme Court.
132	Appellate jurisdiction of Supreme Court in appeals from High Courts in certain cases.	DeMoN needs Appellate jurisdiction of Supreme court from High Courts in certain cases.
133	Appellate jurisdiction of Supreme Court in appeals from High Courts in regard to civil matters.	TaMaM civil matters ke appellate jurisdiction supreme courts se high court gaye.
134	Appellate jurisdiction of Supreme Court in regard to criminal matters.	ToMaR criminal matters appellate jurisdication supreme court ko diya.
134A	Certificate for appeal to the Supreme Court.	ToMaR Alpha bola certificate of appeal le aao supreme court se.
135	Jurisdiction and powers of the Federal Court under existing law to be exercisable by the Supreme	TaMiL gives jurisdiction and power of federal

	Court.	court to be exercise by supreme court.
136	Special leave to appeal by the Supreme Court.	DiMaG se special leave appeal kar supreme court se.
137	Review of judgments or orders by the Supreme Court.	DeeMaK reviews the judgment or orders by the supreme court.
138	Enlargement of the jurisdiction of the Supreme Court.	DoMVa has enlarged the jurisdiction of supreme court.
139	Conferment on the Supreme Court of powers to issue certain writs.	TeMPo give power to supreme court to issue certain writs.
139A	Transfer of certain cases.	TeMPo Aplha use to Transfer certain cases.
140	Ancillary powers of Supreme Court.	ToRSo has ancillary power of supreme court.
141	Law declared by Supreme Court to be binding on all courts.	TReaT for Law declared by supreme court be binding on all courts.
142	Enforcement of decrees and orders of Supreme Court and orders as to discovery, etc.	Supreme court has TRaiN of Decree.
143	Power of President to consult Supreme Court.	DRaMa has given power to president to consult supreme court.
144	Civil and judicial authorities to act in aid of the Supreme Court.	DaRaR banta hai, when civil and judicial authorities act in aid of supreme court.
145	Rules of Court, etc.	TRiaL the rule of court.

146	Officers and servants and the expenses of the Supreme Court.	TRaSH officers and servants and the expenses of the supreme court.
147	Interpretation.	TReaK needs Interpretation.
148	Comptroller and Auditor-General of India.	DRiVe cars of Comptroller and Auditor-General of India.
149	Duties and powers of the Comptroller and Auditor-General.	DRoP the duties and Power of Controller and Auditor-General.
150	Form of accounts of the Union and of the States.	TaLeS form account of union and state.
151	Audit reports.	ToiLeT ka Audit Reports dikhao.

PART VI
THE STATES

152	Definition.	TaLNe se state define hota hai.

THE EXECUTIVE
The Governor

153	Governors of States.	TaLiM Milti hai state Governer se.
154	Executive power of State.	TaiLoR state ka executive power silta hai.
155	Appointment of Governor.	DaLaL steet pe Governor appoint hote hai.

156	Term of office of Governor.	DiaLoGue marke ke Governor ke office ka term batao.
157	Qualifications for appointment as Governor.	TiLaK se governor ke appointment ka qualfication pata chalta hai.
158	Conditions of Governor's office.	SeLFi ke liye Governor's office ki condition manni padegi.
159	Oath or affirmation by the Governor.	TuLiP is need for taking oath or affirmation by the governor.
160	Discharge of the functions of the Governor in certain contingencies.	TaGS Discharge of the functions of Governor in certain contingencies.
161	Power of Governor to grant pardons, etc., and to suspend, remit or commute sentences in certain cases.	DiGiT Me pardons grant karta hai Governor.
162	Extent of executive power of State.	DiGeNe extends executive power of state.
Council of Ministers		
163	Council of Ministers to aid and advise Governor.	DoGMa of council of ministers to aid and advise Governor.
164	Other provisions as to Ministers.	TiGeR gets others provisions as to ministers.
The Advocate-General for the State		

165	Advocate-General for the State.	DoGLa goes to Advocate-General of the state.
Conduct of Government Business		
166	Conduct of business of the Government of a State.	DiGG into the conduct of business of the Government of a state.
167	Duties of Chief Minister as respects the furnishing of information to Governor, etc.	TaGiC duties of chief miniter furnishing information to Govornor.
THE STATE LEGISLATURE		
168	Constitution of Legislatures in States	I came ToGiVe lecture on costitution of legislatures in state.
169	Abolition or creation of Legislative Councils in States.	TeaGaP is needed before Abolition or Creation of Legislative councils in states.
170	Composition of the Legislative Assemblies.	It TaKeS effort to do the composition of the legislative assemblies.
171	Composition of the Legislative Councils.	DiCT have composition of legislative council
172	Duration of State Legislatures.	DuKaN me State Legislature a duration latka hai.
173	Qualification for membership of the State Legislature.	DiCoM has published the qualification for the membership of state Legislature.

174	Sessions of the State Legislature, prorogation and dissolution.	DeeKRa hold the sessiom of state legislature i.e prorogation and dissolution.
175	Right of Governor to address and send messages to the House or Houses.	TakLa Governor has right to address and send message to the house.
176	Special address by the Governor.	TaKeShi castle has special address by the Governor.
177	Rights of Ministers and Advocate-General as respects the Houses.	TiKKa orders rights of ministers and Advocate-General as respects the houses.
Officers of the State Legislature		
178	The Speaker and Deputy Speaker of the Legislative Assembly.	DeKoF Total hai to speaker and deputy speaker Legislative Assembly me hai.
179	Vacation and resignation of, and removal from, the offices of Speaker and Deputy Speaker.	TCP sends Vacation and resignation from the offices of Speaker and deputy speaker.
180	Power of the Deputy Speaker or other person to perform the duties of the office of, or to act as, Speaker.	TVS give power to Deputy speaker to act as speaker
181	The Speaker or the Deputy Speaker not to preside while a resolution for his removal from office is under consideration.	DVD has recorded that speaker and deputy speaker not to preside when removal from

		office is under consideration.
182	The Chairman and Deputy Chairman of the Legislative Council.	TooFaN Chairman or deputy chairman ko Legislative council le gaya.
183	Vacation and resignation of, and removal from, the offices of Chairman and Deputy Chairman.	DeFaMe will vacate the office of Chairman and deputy chairman.
184	Power of the Deputy Chairman or other person to perform the duties of the office of, or to act as, Chairman.	DeVaR gives power to deputy chairman to act as chairman.
185	The Chairman or the Deputy Chairman not to preside while a resolution for his removal from office is under consideration.	DeViL will not allow chairman and deputy chairman to preside if their removal is under consideration.
186	Salaries and allowances of the Speaker and Deputy Speaker and the Chairman and Deputy Chairman.	DeFoG will clear salaries and allowances of speaker , Deputy speaker, chairman and deputy chairman.
187	Secretariat of State Legislature.	DeViKa ko state legislature ka secretariate mila hai.
Conduct of Business		
188	Oath or affirmation by members.	TVF shows Oath and affirmation by members for conducting business.

		Note : DeFF can also be used.
189	Voting in Houses, power of Houses to act notwithstanding vacancies and quorum.	DeVaPi did voting in Houses and gain power of houses to act notwithstanding vacancies and quorum.

Disqualifications of Members

190	Vacation of seats.	ToPaZ vacate the seat of disqualified members.
191	Disqualifications for membership.	DeBiT card not available for Disqualified members.
192	Decision on questions as to disqualifications of members.	DeePeN thoughts helps to make decision on questions regarding disqualifications of members.
193	Penalty for sitting and voting before making oath or affirmation under article 188 or when not qualified or when disqualified.	DeePaM shows penalty if you votes without oath under TVF or when disqualified or not qualified

Powers, privileges and immunities of State Legislatures and their Members

194	Powers, privileges, etc., of the Houses of Legislatures and of the members and committees thereof.	DiPeR pehnenge to power , privileges milega aapke state ke house of legislature , members and committees ko.

195	Salaries and allowances of members.	DiPoLe bhi state ki salaries aur allowances se charge rehte hai.
	Legislative Procedure	
196	Provisions as to introduction and passing of Bills.	DeePeSH state me bill introduce aur pass karne ka provision pata hai.
197	Restriction on powers of Legislative Council as to Bills other than Money Bills.	DiPiKa put restriction on power of Legislative council as to bill other than money bill.
198	Special procedure in respect of Money Bills.	TiPoVa village know the special procedure in respect of money bill.
199	Definition of "Money Bills".	DiBBe me Money bill ka defination hai.
200	Assent to Bills.	NaSSau gives assent to Legislative bills.
201	Bills reserved for consideration.	INSTa reseves bill for consideration.
	Procedure in Financial Matters	
202	Annual financial statement.	INSaN annual fianancial statement se hamesha pareshan reshta hai.
203	Procedure in Legislature with respect to estimates.	NaZiM check procedure in

		legislature w.r.t estimation.
204	Appropriation Bills.	NaSooR ban jaata hai Appropriation bill.
205	Supplementary, additional or excess grants.	NaSaL se pata chalta hai ki supplementray ya excess grants chahiye.
206	Votes on account, votes of credit and exceptional grants.	NaaSaaj hojate hai jab vote on account, credit ya exceptional grant ka karte hai tab.
207	Special provisions as to financial Bills.	NuSKa lagta hai financial bill ke special provision ke liye.
	Procedure Generally	
208	Rules of procedure.	INSaaF, Rule of Procedure se hi milega.
209	Regulation by law of procedure in the Legislature of the State in relation to financial business.	NaSeeB se regulation aur law bana hai state legislature ke financial business ko leke.
210	Language to be used in the Legislature.	ANDaZ se language use hota hai legislature me. Note: iNDUS
211	Restriction on discussion in the Legislature.	INDeeD , restriction on discussion in legislature is required.
212	Courts not to inquire into proceedings of the Legislature.	INDIAN courts cannot inquire into proceedings of the Legislature.

<table>
<tr><td colspan="3" align="center">LEGISLATIVE POWER OF THE GOVERNOR</td></tr>
<tr><td>213</td><td>Power of Governor to promulgate Ordinances during recess of Legislature.</td><td>ANTiM power governor ke pass hai jo Ordinances promulgate kar sakta hai Legislature ke recess me.</td></tr>
<tr><td colspan="3" align="center">THE HIGH COURTS IN THE STATES</td></tr>
<tr><td>214</td><td>High Courts for States.</td><td>NaTuRe has High courts for states.</td></tr>
<tr><td>215</td><td>High Courts to be courts of record.</td><td>NooDLe made high court as a court of record.</td></tr>
<tr><td>216</td><td>Constitution of High Courts.</td><td>NeTaJi declared constitution of high courts.</td></tr>
<tr><td>217</td><td>Appointment and conditions of the office of a Judge of a High Court.</td><td>NaaTaK hota hai high court judge ke appointment aur office conditions ko leke.</td></tr>
<tr><td>218</td><td>Application of certain provisions relating to Supreme Court to High Courts.</td><td>NaTiVe gave application of certain provisions relating supreme court to high court.</td></tr>
<tr><td>219</td><td>Oath or affirmation by Judges of High Courts.</td><td>NaDiPe high court ke judges Oatha aur Affirmation lete hai.</td></tr>
<tr><td>220</td><td>Restriction on practice after being a permanent Judge.</td><td>ANaaNuS put restriction on practice after being a permanent judge.</td></tr>
</table>

221	Salaries, etc., of Judges.	NaNDi high court ke judges ki salary deta hai.
222	Transfer of a Judge from one High Court to another.	ANNaNe judges ko ek high court se dusre high court me trasfer kiya.
223	Appointment of acting Chief Justice.	NaNiMa acting chief justice ko appoint karti hai.
224	Appointment of additional and acting Judges.	NooNeR appoints additional and acting judges.
224A	Appointment of retired Judges at sittings of High Courts.	NooNeR Alpha appoints retired judges at sittings of High courts.
225	Jurisdiction of existing High Courts.	ANNuaL jurisdiction of existing High courts.
226	Power of High Courts to issue certain writs.	NaNGa power hota hai high courts ke pass to issue certain writs.
227	Power of superintendence over all courts by the High Court.	NaaNak has power to superintendence over all courts by high courts.
228	Transfer of certain cases to High Court.	INNoVa used to Transfer certain cases to High court.
229	Officers and servants and the expenses of High Courts.	NaNo-P has officers, servants and expenses of high courts.
230	Extension of jurisdiction of High Courts to Union territories.	NaMaZ extend jurisdiction of high courts to union territories.

231	Establishment of a common High Court for two or more States.	NiMoDa establish common high court for two or more states.
232	Articles 230, 231 and 232 substituted by articles 230 and 231	NaMaN to article 230, 231 and 232 which is substituted by article 230 and 231.
233	Appointment of district judges.	NaMaMi appoint districts judges.
233A	Validation of appointments of, and judgments, etc., delivered by, certain district judges.	NaMaMi Alpha validate appointments, judgments delivered by certain district judges.
234	Recruitment of persons other than district judges to the judicial service.	NoMoRe recruitment of person other than district judges to the judicial services.
235	Control over subordinate courts.	ANMoL control over subordinate courts.
236	Interpretation.	NaMCha hills keeps interpretation.
237	Application of the provisions of this Chapter to certain class or classes of magistrates.	NaMaK puts application of the provision of this chapter to certain class or classes of magistrates.
	PART VII- [Omitted] THE STATES IN PART B OF THE FIRST SCHEDULE	
238	-Omitted	
	PART VIII THE UNION TERRITORIES	

239	Administration of Union territories.	NaMiBia administer union territories.
239A	Creation of local Legislatures or Council of Ministers or both for certain Union territories.	NaMiBia Alpha look after creation of legislature, council of minister or both for union territories.
239AA	Special provisions with respect to Delhi.	NaMiBia Alpha Alpha holds special provision w.r.t Delhi.
239AB	Provision in case of failure of constitutional machinery.	NaMiBia Alpha Beta grab provision in case of failure of constitutional machinery.
239B	Power of administrator to promulgate Ordinances during recess of Legislature.	NaMiBia Beta you have power to promulgate ordinance during recess of legislature.
240	Power of President to make regulations for certain Union territories.	NaRSo president will get power to make regulation for certain union territories.
241	High Courts for Union territories.	NaRuTo created High courts for Union Territories.
242	Coorg--Omitted.	NooRaNi

PART IX
THE PANCHAYATS

243	Definitions.	NiRMa panchayat ki definition hai.
243A	Gram Sabha.	NiRMa Aplha Garam sabha hai

243B	Constitution of Panchayats.	NiRMa Beta Tu panchayat ka consitution hai.
243C	Composition of Panchayats.	NiRMa Charlie you compose panchayat songs
243D	Reservation of seats.	NiRMa Delta reserve panchayat seats
243E	Duration of Panchayats, etc.	NiRMa Echo the duration of panchayats
243F	Disqualifications for membership.	NiRMa Fox smartly disqualify members of panchayat
243G	Powers, authority and responsibilities of Panchayats.	NiRMa Golf plays with power, authority and responsibility of panchayats
243H	Powers to impose taxes by, and Funds of, the Panchayats.	NiRMa Hotel impose taxes of fund of the panchayats
243I	Constitution of Finance Commission to review financial position.	NiRMa India has Constitution of finance and Commission to review financial position.
243J	Audit of accounts of Panchayats.	NiRMa Juliet you audit the accounts of Panchayats.
243K	Elections to the Panchayats.	NiRMa Kilo weighs the election of panchayats.
243L	Application to Union territories.	NiRMa Lima give application to union territories.
243M	Part not to apply to certain areas.	NiRMa Mike keep the parts not apply to certain areas.

243N	Continuance of existing laws and Panchayats.	NiRMa November will continue the existing law and panchayats.
243O	Bar to interference by courts in electoral matters.	NiRMa Oscar bar will interfere by courts in electoral matters.

PART IXA
THE MUNICIPALITIES

243P	Definitions.	NiRMa Papa defines municipalities.
243Q	Constitution of Municipalities.	NiRMa Quebec constitute municipality
243R	Composition of Municipalities.	NiRMa Romeo compose municipality song.
243S	Constitution and composition of Wards Committees, etc.	NiRMa Sierra constitute and compose wards committees.
243T	Reservation of seats.	NiRMa Tango reserve seats for municipality
243U	Duration of Municipalities, etc.	NiRMa Uniform require till the duration of muncipality.
243V	Disqualifications for membership.	NiRMa Victor will disqualify municipality members.
243W	Powers, authority and responsibilities of Municipalities, etc.	NiRMa whisky is risky for power, authority and responsibility of municipalities.
243X	Power to impose taxes by, and Funds of, the Municipalities.	NiRMa X-Ray powers to impose taxes and funds of municipalities.

243Y	Finance Commission.	NiRMa Yankee funky finance commission of municipalities.
243Z	Audit of accounts of Municipalities.	NiRMa Zulu audit the accounts of municipalities.
243ZA	Elections to the Municipalities.	NiRMa Zulu Alpha keep eye on election of muncipalities.
243ZB	Application to Union territories.	NiRMa Zulu Beta prepare application to union territories of municipalities.
243ZC	Part not to apply to certain areas.	NiRMa Zulu Charlie Chapline part not to apply in certain areas of municipalities.
243ZD	Committee for district planning.	NiRMa Zulu Delta deals committee for district planning.
243ZE	Committee for Metropolitan planning.	NiRMa Zulu Echo the committee for metropolitan planning in municipalities.
243ZF	Continuance of existing laws and Municipalities.	NiRMa Zulu Fox make smart move to continue existing laws and municipalities.
243ZG	Bar to interference by courts in electoral matters.	NiRMa Zulu Golf opened bar to interfere by courts in electoral matters of municipalities.

PART IXB
THE CO-OPERATIVE SOCIETIES

243ZH	Definitions.	NiRMa Zulu Hotel has also defined co-operative societies.
243ZI	Incorporation of co-operative societies.	NiRMa Zulu India incorporated co-operative societies.
243ZJ	Number and term of members of board and its office bearers.	NiRMa Zulu Juliet count the number and terms of board members and it's office bearers.
243ZK	Election of members of board.	NiRMa Zulu kilo weight the board member election.
243ZL	Supersession and suspension of board and interim management.	NiRMa Zulu Lima you supress and suspend board and interim management.
243ZM	Audit of accounts of co-operative societies.	NiRMa Zulu Mike do the audit of accounts of co-operative societies.
243ZN	Convening of general body meetings.	NiRMa Zulu November is convening of general body meetings.
243ZO	Right of a member to get information.	NiRMa Zulu Oscar given the right of a member to get information.
243ZP	Returns.	NiRMa Zulu Papa give returns to co-operative societies.
243ZQ	Offences and penalties.	NiRMa Zulu Quebec the offences and penalties on co-operative societies.

243ZR	Application to multi-State co-operative societies.	NiRMa Zulu Romeo rome to give application to multi state co-operative societies.
243ZS	Application to Union territories.	NiRMa Zulu Sierra can write application to union territories
243ZT	Continuance of existing laws.	NiRMa Zulu Tango enforce the continuance of existing laws of co-operative societies.

<table>
<tr><td colspan="3" align="center">PART X
THE SCHEDULED AND TRIBAL AREAS</td></tr>
</table>

244	Administration of Scheduled Areas and Tribal Areas.	NaRaRa administer scheduled areas and Tribal areas
244A	Formation of an autonomous State comprising certain tribal areas in Assam and creation of local Legislature or Council of Ministers or both therefor.	NaRaRa Alpha can formed an autonomous state comprising certain tribal areas in Assam and creation of local legislature or council of Ministers or Both therefor.

<table>
<tr><td colspan="3" align="center">PART XI
RELATIONS BETWEEN THE UNION AND THE STATES
LEGISLATIVE RELATIONS
Distribution of Legislative Powers</td></tr>
</table>

245	Extent of laws made by Parliament and by the Legislatures of States.	NiRaLi extent law made by parliament

		and by the legislature of states.
246	Subject-matter of laws made by Parliament and by the Legislatures of States.	NaRaChi is a subject matter of laws made by parliament and by the legislature of states.
247	Power of Parliament to provide for the establishment of certain additional courts.	NaRaK gives power to parliament to provide for the establishment of certain additional courts.
248	Residuary powers of legislation.	NeeRaV has residuary power of legislation.
249	Power of Parliament to legislate with respect to a matter in the State List in the national interest.	NaiRoBi provides power to parliament to legislate w.r.t a matter in the state list in the national interest.
250	Power of Parliament to legislate with respect to any matter in the State List if a Proclamation of Emergency is in operation.	NaiLS have so much power of parliament to legislate w.r.t any matter in the state list if a proclamation of Emergency is in operation.
251	Inconsistency between laws made by Parliament under articles 249 and 250 and laws made by the Legislatures of States.	INLeT the Inconsistency between laws made by parliament under article 249 and 250 and laws made by legislature of State.
252	Power of Parliament to legislate for two or more States by consent and adoption of such legislation by any other State.	INLiNe the power of parliament to legislate for two or more state by consent and

		adoption of such legislation by any other state.
253	Legislation for giving effect to international agreements.	NeeLaM stone jaruri hai internation agreements ko effect me lane ke liyea.
254	Inconsistency between laws made by Parliament and laws made by the Legislatures of States.	NaLaRa inconsistency between laws made by parliament and laws made by legislature of state
255	Requirements as to recommendations and previous sanctions to be regarded as matters of procedure only.	NaLLa gives requirements as to recommendations and previous sanctions to be regarded as matters of procedure.
ADMINISTRATIVE RELATIONS		
256	Obligation of States and the Union.	ANALOG is the Obligation of states and the Union.
257	Control of the Union over States in certain cases.	State UNLiKe the control of the union over in certain cases
258	Power of the Union to confer powers, etc., on States in certain cases.	INLoVe with power of union to confer powers on state in certain cases.
258A	Power of the States to entrust functions to the Union.	INLoVe Alpha with power of the state to entrust function to the union.
259	Omitted	

260	Jurisdiction of the Union in relation to territories outside India.	NaChoS khao aur india ke bahar ki territories ke liye union ki jurisdiction badhao.
261	Public acts, records and judicial proceedings.	NaShTa me bana hai public acts, records aur judicial proceedings. Note : NaGaaDa
	Disputes relating to Waters	
262	Adjudication of disputes relating to waters of inter-State rivers or river valleys. Co-ordination between States	NaGiN ke inter state river ya vally me ja ke nayaik nirnay (Adjudicate)de sakti hai.
263	Provisions with respect to an inter-State Council.	ANJaaM bura hoga agar inter-state provision nahi accept kiya to.
	PART XII **FINANCE, PROPERTY, CONTRACTS AND SUITS.** **FINANCE**	
264	Interpretation.	NiGRo has interpretation of finance, property,contracts and suits finance.
265	Taxes not to be imposed save by authority of law.	NaSheeLa Taxes not be imposed saved by authority of law.
266	Consolidated Funds and public accounts of India and of the States.	NaGaJi India aur State ke consolidated aur

		public funds ko aapne pass rakhiye.
267	Contingency Fund.	NaJuk hote hai india contingency fund.

Distribution of Revenues between the Union and the States

268	Duties levied by the Union but collected and appropriated by the State.	INGaVa duties levide by union but collected and appropriated by stated.
269	Taxes levied and collected by the Union but assigned to the States.	NaGoBa collects taxes levied by union but assigned by states.
270	Taxes levied and distributed between the Union and the States.	INKS write the taxes levied and distributed between union and the state.
271	Surcharge on certain duties and taxes for purposes of the Union.	ANekTa hogi to you wil pay surcharge on certain duties and texes for purposes of the union.
272	Omitted	
273	Grants in lieu of export duty on jute and jute products.	NaKaaM hoga to export duty bharega jute aur jute products pe.
274	Prior recommendation of President required to Bills affecting taxation in which States are interested.	NauKaR bola jo bill tax ko affect karega jisme states interested hai uske liye pior recommendation lagega.

		Note: iNKaR
275	Grants from the Union to certain States.	NaKLi Grants union se milta hai to certain states
276	Taxes on professions, trades, callings and employments.	ANKuSh lagao profession , trades, callings and empleyment taxes pe.
277	Savings.	NCC state aur union ke savings ko guard karte hai
278	Omitted	
279	Calculation of "net proceeds", etc.	NaKaaB se calculation karte hai "Net Prceeds" ko.
280	Finance Commission.	NaVaZ finance comission chalata hai
281	Recommendations of the Finance Commission.	InViTe recommendations of the finance commission. Note : INVaDe

Miscellaneous financial provisions

282	Expenditure defrayable by the Union or a State out of its revenues.	NaVeeN kuch defrayeble expenditures union or state ke revenue se leta hai.
283	Custody, etc., of Consolidated Funds, Contingency Funds and moneys credited to the public accounts.	NaVaM ke custody me Consolidate funds, Contingency Funds aur public accounts me credited paise hai.

284	Custody of suitors' deposits and other moneys received by public servants and courts.	NeFRo ke custody me suitor's deposits aur public servants aur court se mile hue paise hai.
285	Exemption of property of the Union from State taxation.	NaVaL exempted the property of union from state taxation. Note: NoVaL
286	Restrictions as to imposition of tax on the sale or purchase of goods.	ANaaVeSh puts restrictions to impose tax on sale or purchase of good.
287	Exemption from taxes on electricity.	INVoiCe is exempted from tax on electricity.
288	Exemption from taxation by States in respect of water or electricity in certain cases.	NViVo received exemption from taxes by state on water or electricity for certain cases.
289	Exemption of property and income of a State from Union taxation.	NaVaB ko union taxation se jo property bani hai aur income bana hai usme exemption mila hai.
290	Adjustment in respect of certain expenses and pensions.	NPS is required for adjustment in certain expenses and pension.
290A	Annual payment to certain Devaswom Funds.	NPS Alpha make annual payment to certain devaswom funds.
291	Privy purse sums of Rulers.-- Omitted.	InPuT

BORROWING		
292	Borrowing by the Government of India.	NaPNa jo bhi Govenment of India ne borrow kiya hai.
293	Borrowing by States.	ANuPaM jimmedar hai state borrowing ke liye.
PROPERTY, CONTRACTS, RIGHTS, LIABILITIES, OBLIGATIONS AND SUITS		
294	Succession to property, assets, rights, liabilities and obligations in certain cases.	NuPuR also has Succession to property, assets, rights, liabilities and obligations in certain cases.
295	Succession to property, assets, rights, liabilities and obligations in other cases.	NePaL has succession to property, assets, rights, liabilities and obligations in other cases. Note: NoBeL
296	Property accruing by escheat or laps or as bona vacantia.	NoPeG for property accruing by escheat or laps or as bona vacantia.
297	Things of value within territorial waters or continental shelf and resources of the exclusive economic zone to vest in the Union.	NaaPaK n irade se mile valuable resources ko union shelf me bhar ke economic zone me le jati hai.

298	Power to carry on trade, etc.	NBF has power to carry trade.
299	Contracts.	NiPPo battery has Contract on Obligations and Suits.
300	Suits and proceedings.	MoSS suits in proceedings

RIGHT TO PROPERTY

300A	Persons not to be deprived of property save by authority of law.	MiSS Aplha your right to property cannot be deprived.

PART XIII
TRADE, COMMERCE AND INTERCOURSE WITHIN THE TERRITORY OF INDIA

301	Freedom of trade, commerce and intercourse.	MaSTi ke liye free me trade , commerce and intercourse hona chahiye.
302	Power of Parliament to impose restrictions on trade, commerce and intercourse.	aMaZoN aayega agar parliament ne aapke trade, commerece aur intercourse pe restriction laga diya to.
303	Restrictions on the legislative powers of the Union and of the States with regard to trade and commerce.	MauSuM ne trade aur commerce ko leke restrictions laga diye union and state ke legislative power pe.
304	Restrictions on trade, commerce and intercourse among States.	MaSooRie me trade,commerce is restricted among states.

Article	Title	Mnemonic
305	Saving of existing laws and laws providing for State monopolies.	MiSaL dete hai hum for saving existing laws and laws providing for state monopolies.
306	Power of certain States in Part B of the First Schedule to impose restrictions on trade and commerce.--Omitted	
307	Appointment of authority for carrying out the purposes of articles 301 to 304.	MuSKa lagata hai to appoint authority for MaSTi to MaSooRie.

PART XIV
SERVICES UNDER THE UNION AND THE STATES.
SERVICES

Article	Title	Mnemonic
308	Interpretation.	MoSoVo interprets services under union and the states.
309	Recruitment and conditions of service of persons serving the Union or a State.	MSP pe recruitment aur conditions decided hote to jo bhi person state ya union ko serve karta hai.
310	Tenure of office of persons serving the Union or a State.	MiDaS king decide tenure of office of person serving in union or state.
311	Dismissal, removal or reduction in rank of persons employed in civil capacities under the Union or a State.	MoTTo required for dismissal, removal or reduction in rank in civil capacity under union or state.
312	All-India services.	MaDiNa me dua kijiye All India Service ke Liye.

Article	Description	Mnemonic
312A	Power of Parliament to vary or revoke conditions of service of officers of certain services.	MaDiNa Alpha gives power to parliament to revoke conditions of service of officers of certain services.
313	Transitional provisions.	MaaTaM manao transitional provisions ke liye. Note: MTM
314	Provision for protection of existing officers of certain services.-- Omitted.	MoToR ko protect karna officers se

PUBLIC SERVICE COMMISSIONS

Article	Description	Mnemonic
315	Public Service Commissions for the Union and for the States.	MeTaL is the base for public service commissions for union and state
316	Appointment and term of office of members.	MaDaGa Lake is filled with Appointment and terms of office of PSC.
317	Removal and suspension of a member of a Public Service Commission.	MaTKa can remove and suspend members of public service commission.
318	Power to make regulations as to conditions of service of members and staff of the Commission.	MoTiF gives power to make regulations for the condition of service of PSC and staff of the commission.
319	Prohibition as to the holding of offices by members of Commission on ceasing to be such members.	AMiTaB Prohibits the holding of offices by member of commission on ceasing to be such members.

320	Functions of Public Service Commissions.	MNS ke haath me public service commission ke functions hai
321	Power to extend functions of Public Service Commissions.	MiND has power to extend functions of PSC.
322	Expenses of Public Service Commissions.	MiNioN increased the expenses of PSC.
323	Reports of Public Service Commissions.	AMoNiuM smells reports of PSC .

PART XIVA
TRIBUNALS

323A	Administrative tribunals.	EMiNeM Alpha tribunals Administer karta hai
323B	Tribunals for other matters.	EMiNeM ka Beta tribunal ke baaki matters dekhta hai

PART XV
ELECTIONS

324	Superintendence, direction and control of elections to be vested in an Election Commission.	MiNoR has vested power to election commission to supritend, direct and control election
325	No person to be ineligible for inclusion in, or to claim to be included in a special, electoral roll on	MaNaLi person is ineligible to include in special electoral for ground of religion, race, cast or sex.

	grounds of religion, race, caste or sex.	
326	Elections to the House of the People and to the Legislative Assemblies of States to be on the basis of adult suffrage.	MaNGo is required for election of house of people & SLA on the basis of adult suffrage.
327	Power of Parliament to make provision with respect to elections to Legislatures.	MaNiaC takes power of parliament to make provision w.r.t elections to legislatures.
328	Power of Legislature of a State to make provision with respect to elections to such Legislature.	MaNaV ne state legislature ko power diya ki wo legislature ke election ko leke provision bana sake.
329	Bar to interference by courts in electoral matters.	MaNPe creates Bar to interfere by courts in electoral matters.
SPECIAL PROVISIONS RELATING TO CERTAIN CLASSES		
330	Reservation of seats for Scheduled Castes and Scheduled Tribes in the House of the People.	MoMoS khake scheduled caste aur scheduled tribes ke seat reserve kiye hai house of people ne.
331	Representation of the Anglo-Indian community in the House of the People.	MaMTa bandhkar Anglo-Indian community ko representation diya house of people ne.

332	Reservation of seats for Scheduled Castes and Scheduled Tribes in the Legislative Assemblies of the States.	MeMNa has reserved seats for SC and ST in Legislative Assemblies of states.
333	Representation of the Anglo-Indian community in the Legislative Assemblies of the States.	MuMMa represents Anglo indian community in the Legislative Assemblies of the states.
334	Reservation of seats and special representation to cease after seventy years.	MaaMRa will cease seats reservation and special representations after 70 years.
335	Claims of Scheduled Castes and Scheduled Tribes to services and posts.	MaMLa schedule caste , Scheduled tribes ke service aur posts ke claims ka hai.
336	Special provision for Anglo-Indian community in certain services.	MaMaJi needs special provision for Anglo-indian community in certail services.
337	Special provision with respect to educational grants for the benefit of Anglo-Indian Community.	MiMiC The special provision w.r.t ecucational grants for the benefit of Anglo-Indian community.
338	National Commission for Scheduled Castes.	aMMa Vo National commission hai SC, ST ke liye.
338A	National Commission for Scheduled Tribes.	aMMa Vo Alpha National commission hai Scheduled Tribes ke liye.
338B	National Commission for Backward Classes.	aMMa Vo Beta

339	Control of the Union over the administration of Scheduled Areas and the welfare of Scheduled Tribes.	MiMBa karke union scheduled Area ka administration aur scheduled tribes ka welfare control karta hai.
340	Appointment of a Commission to investigate the conditions of backward classes.	MaRZi se commission appoint karta hu backward class ki condition investigate karne ke liye. Note:MiRZa
341	Scheduled Castes.	MuRaaD se scheduled caste hai. Note : MaRD
342	Scheduled Tribes.	MaRiNa beach have special provision scheduled tribes.
342A	Socially and educationally backward classes.	MaRiNa – Alpha is socially and educationally backward classes.

PART XVII
OFFICIAL LANGUAGE.
LANGUAGE OF THE UNION

| 343 | Official language of the Union. | MeRi-Ma ki language union ki official language hai.

Note:MaRiuM MuRMu |
| 344 | Commission and Committee of Parliament on official language. | MuRaRi named commission and committee of |

		parliament on official language.
<td colspan="3" align="center">REGIONAL LANGUAGES</td>
345	Official language or languages of a State.	MuRLi jaisi state ki official language hai.
346	Official language for communication between one State and another or between a State and the Union.	MuRGa speaks official language between two states or union and the state.
347	Special provision relating to language spoken by a section of the population of a State.	MaRCo uses special provision related to language spoken by a section of the population.
<td colspan="3" align="center">LANGUAGE OF THE SUPREME COURT, HIGH COURTS, ETC.</td>
348	Language to be used in the Supreme Court and in the High Courts and for Acts, Bills, etc.	MuRFi is the language for Supreme court, high court and for Acts and bills etc.
349	Special procedure for enactment of certain laws relating to language.	MRP is special procedure for enactment of certain laws relating to language.
<td colspan="3" align="center">SPECIAL DIRECTIVES</td>

350	Language to be used in representations for redress of grievances.	MoLeS knows the language to be used in representation for redress of grievances.
350A	Facilities for instruction in mother-tongue at primary stage.	MoLeS Alpha provides facilities for instruction in mother tongue at primary stage.
350B	Special Officer for linguistic minorities.	MoLeS Beta tum special officer ho linguistic minorities ke.
351	Directive for development of the Hindi language.	MaLaDi is directive for development of hindi language. MaLaD

PART XVIII
EMERGENCY PROVISIONS

352	Proclamation of Emergency.	MiLo-Na National Emergency me.
353	Effect of Proclamation of Emergency.	MaLuM hai kya effect hota emergency proclamation ka.
354	Application of provisions relating to distribution of revenues while a Proclamation of Emergency is in operation.	MoLaR puts application of provision regarding revenue distribution while emergency proclamation is in operation.
355	Duty of the Union to protect States against external aggression and internal disturbance.	MaLaaL hai ki union state ko protect kart hai external aggression ya internal disturbance se.

356	Provisions in case of failure of constitutional machinery in States.	MiL-Ja state emergency se (President rule)
357	Exercise of legislative powers under Proclamation issued under article 356.	MaLiK Exercise legislative power under proclamation issued under(article 356) MiLJa.
358	Suspension of provisions of article 19 during emergencies.	MoLVi suspends the article 19(TaP) during emergencies. Note : You can also read it as "MoLVi suspends Tap during emergencies"
359	Suspension of the enforcement of the rights conferred by Part III during emergencies.	MaLBa suspends the rights conferred by part III during emergencies. Note : MaLiBu
360	Provisions as to financial emergency	MuJSe finnancial emergency ki permission let hai sab.

PART XIX

MISCELLANEOUS

361	Protection of President and Governors and Rajpramukhs.	MaGeT Protects President and Governor.
361A	Protection of publication of proceedings of Parliament and State Legislatures.	MaGeT Alpha Protects the publication of Parliamentary proceeding and state legislature.

Article	Description	Mnemonic
361B	Disqualification for appointment on remunerative political post.	MaGeT Beta deals with disqualification for appointment of remunarative political post.
362	Rights and privileges of Rulers of Indian States.--Omitted.	MaJNu
363	Bar to interference by courts in disputes arising out of certain treaties, agreements, etc.	MaGaR has bar to interfere by court in disputes of certain treaties and agreement.
363A	Recognition granted to Rulers of Indian States to cease and privy purses to be abolished.	MaGaR Alpha Recognition granted to Rulers of Indian States to cease and privy purses to be abolished.
364	Special provisions as to major ports and aerodromes.	MaJoR sahab holds special provisions to major prots and Aerodromes.
365	Effect of failure to comply with, or to give effect to, directions given by the Union.	MaJaaL hi koi union ke direction comply na kare.
366	Definitions.	MaGGie masala has miscellaneous definations.
367	Interpretation.	MiGiC interprets miscellaneous.

PART XX

AMENDMENT OF THE CONSTITUTION

368	Power of Parliament to amend the Constitution and procedure therefore.	MuJVa me constitution ammend karte hai

<table>
<tr><td colspan="3" align="center">PART XXI
TEMPORARY, TRANSITIONAL AND SPECIAL PROVISIONS</td></tr>
</table>

Article	Description	Mnemonic
369	Temporary power to Parliament to make laws with respect to certain matters in the State List as if they were matters in the Concurrent List.	MaGPie bird give temporary powers to parliament to make law w.r.t certain matter in the state list as if they were matter in concurrent list.
370	Temporary provisions with respect to the State of Jammu and Kashmir.	MaCoS(MacOs) has temprory provision w.r.t state of J & K.
371	Special provision with respect to the States of Maharashtra and Gujarat.	McD(short form for MacDonald's) has special provision w.r.t maharashtra & Gujrat.
371A	Special provision with respect to the State of Nagaland.	McD Alpha given special provision w.r.t Nagaland.
371B	Special provision with respect to the State of Assam.	McD Beta has special provision w.r.t Assam.
371C	Special provision with respect to the State of Manipur.	McD Charlie needs special provision w.r.t Manipur.
371D	Special provisions with respect to the State of Andhra Pradesh or the State of Telangana	McD Delta deals with special provision w.r.t Andhra Pradesh or Telangana.

371E	Establishment of Central University in Andhra Pradesh.	McD Echo edited establishment of central university in Andhra Pradesh.
371F	Special provisions with respect to the State of Sikkim.	McD fox hunted special provision w.r.t Sikkim
371G	Special provision with respect to the State of Mizoram.	McD Golf hits special provision w.r.t Mizoram.
371H	Special provision with respect to the State of Arunachal Pradesh.	McD Hotel stayed with special provision w.r.t Arunachal Pradesh.
371I	Special provision with respect to the State of Goa.	McD India shines with special provision w.r.t Goa.
371J	Special provisions with respect to the State of Karnataka.	McD Juliet loves special provision w.r.t Karnataka.
372	Continuance in force of existing laws and their adaptation.	MaKaN (house) continue in force of existing law and their adaptation.
372A	Power of the President to adapt laws.	MaKaN Alpha gives power to president to adapt law.
373	Power of President to make order in respect of persons under preventive detention in certain cases.	MuKaM aisa hai president ka that he has power to make order in respect of person under preventive detection in certain cases.
374	Provisions as to Judges of the Federal Court and proceedings pending in the Federal Court or before His Majesty in Council.	MaCRo has provision for judges of federal court and proceeding pending.

375	Courts, authorities and officers to continue to function subject to the provisions of the Constitution.	MaiKaL hills can ask court , authorities and officer to function subject to the provision of the constitution.
376	Provisions as to Judges of High Courts.	MoKSha provisions the judges of High Courts.
377	Provisions as to Comptroller and Auditor-General of India.	MeCCa ka provisions comptroller and Auditor- General of India ke liye hai.
378	Provisions as to Public Service Commissions.	MaKeuP to create provision as to Public Service Commissions.
378A	Special provision as to duration of Andhra Pradesh Legislative Assembly.	MakeuP Alpha get special provision as to duration of Andhra Pradesh legislative assembly.
379	Provisions as to provisional Parliament and the Speaker and Deputy Speaker thereof -Omitted.	MCB
380	Provision as to President. Omitted.	
381	Council of Ministers of the President.- Omitted.	MuFaT
382	Provisions as to provisional Legislatures for States in Part A of the First Schedule. -- Omitted.	
383	Provision as to Governors of Provinces. -- Omitted.	

384	Council of Ministers of the Governors.--Omitted.	
385	Provision as to provisional Legislatures in States in Part B of the First Schedule.--Omitted.	
386	Council of Ministers for States in Part B of the First Schedule. - - Omitted.	
387	Special provision as to determination of population for the purposes of certain elections.--Omitted.	
388	Provisions as to the filling of casual vacancies in the provisional Parliament and provisional Legislatures of the States.--Omitted.	
389	Provision as to Bills pending in the Dominion Legislatures and 29 in the Legislatures of Provinces and Indian States.--Omitted.	
390	Money received or raised or expenditure incurred between the commencement of the Constitution and the 31st day of March, 1950. --Omitted.	
391	Power of the President to amend the First and Fourth Schedules in certain contingencies.--Omitted.	
392	Power of the President to remove difficulties.	MoVeN the power of the president to remove difficulties.

PART XXII

SHORT TITLE, COMMENCEMENT, AUTHORITATIVE TEXT

IN HINDI AND REPEALS		
393	Short title.	MPM is short title
394	Commencement.	AMPeRe Commencement.
394A	Authoritative text in the Hindi language.	AMPeRe Alpha has authoritative text in hindi langauage.
395	Repeals.	AMPle Repeals

A Message to My Readers

Congratulations on completing this journey of exploring and mastering the articles of our Constitution! Understanding these foundational principles is not just a matter of academic knowledge but a step toward becoming a more informed and responsible citizen.

I hope the tricks and techniques shared in this book have made learning easier, more engaging, and memorable for you.

As you move forward, remember:

- Knowledge grows when shared. Share what you've learned with others to inspire curiosity and awareness.
- The Constitution is a living document. Stay curious, keep learning, and continue exploring how it evolves to meet the needs of our society.
- Your understanding can spark change. Use it to contribute positively to your community and beyond.

Thank you for allowing me to be a part of your learning journey. Your feedback, experiences, and suggestions are invaluable, so don't hesitate to reach out.

Stay curious, stay informed, and stay inspired!

Let's Stay Connected!

Thank you for taking the time to explore this book. Your journey doesn't end here! Let's continue learning and growing together.

Stay updated with more tricks, tips, and valuable content by connecting with me on:

📺 **YouTube**: iStudyUPSC

Follow my channel for insightful videos, strategies, and tips to master constitutional articles and more.

📷 **Instagram**: @istudyupsc

Join me on Instagram for quick updates, engaging posts, and behind-the-scenes learning moments.

Your feedback, questions, and ideas mean a lot to me. Let's build a community of learners who inspire each other!

Looking forward to connecting with you.

ALL THE BEST TO FUTURE IAS AND IPS OFFICERS !!